Conversation Skills:

How to Use Storytelling in Your Communication to Gain Recognition, Be More Likeable, & Connect with People

Keith Coleman

Copyright © 2018 by Keith Coleman

All rights reserved. No part of this publication may be reproduced, distributed, or transmitted in any form or by any means, including photocopying, recording, or other electronic or mechanical methods, without the prior written permission of the publisher, except in the case of brief quotations embodied in critical reviews and certain other non-commercial uses permitted by copyright law.

Furthermore, the information in the following pages is broadly considered to be a truthful and accurate account of facts and such any inattention, use or misuse of the information in question by the reader will render any resulting actions solely under their purview. There are no scenarios in which the publisher or the original author of this work can be in any fashion deemed liable for any hardship or damages that may befall them after undertaking information described herein.

Additionally, the information in the following pages is intended only for informational purposes and should thus be thought of as universal. As befitting its nature, it is presented without assurance regarding its prolonged validity or interim quality. Trademarks that are mentioned are done without written consent and can in no way be considered an endorsement from the trademark holder.

Please contact the author at

keith.coleman@narugipublishing.com

for feedback, omissions or errors regarding the book.

Table of Contents

Introduction 5

Chapter One: Elements of a Compelling and Unforgettable Conversation 9

Chapter Two: Use the Power of Storytelling to Connect with People 29

What Are the Basic Elements of a Good Story? 37

Chapter Three: Weave Stories Effectively in Conversations 43

Chapter Four: Elements of a Powerful Story 57

Chapter Five: Pointers for Narrating Powerful Anecdotes 69

Chapter Six: Using Storytelling for Sales, Business and Professional Networking 85

Using Anecdotes in Speeches and Presentations 95

Using Story Telling in Training 99

Conclusion 101

>>GET A FREE & EXCLUSIVE SELF-DISCIPLINE COPY<<

To instantly download **a free copy of Self-Discipline** – "5 powerful steps to refill motivation and practice self-control" **not available elsewhere**,

Visit: **http://bit.ly/displin**

Introduction

Go back to the time when you met someone for the first time and came back completely blown away by the conversation. You were most likely so captivated that you didn't want the conversation to end. Think about what the conversationalist did to keep you hooked to the interaction? Did they merely state facts, figures, statistics and research to keep the conversation going? I bet not! Chances are they used the power of relatable, compelling and interesting stories and personal accounts to get across their point.

Who doesn't love listening to an engaging and captivating personal account of stories? It makes the storyteller more likable and identifiable. While listening to them, you are almost tempted to scream, "Hey, this sounds like me." As humans, we relate wonderfully well to stories on a deeper, subconscious level. It connects or links us to another person by identifying a common thread.

Take, for instance, you are struggling to keep a job and constantly switching careers or at a point where you are confused whether to give up a secure job to follow your passion. You share this with an acquaintance. He/she then advises you about following your passion, and it is the best thing you can do for yourself. They go on about how you can build a rewarding and profitable career out of it. You come back even more confused after the suggestions!

Contrast this with an acquaintance sharing a powerful story about his/her friend in a similar situation which includes everything, why the friends took a tough decision to quit his/her job, how they managed to keep aside some security funds until he/she worked to build a successful career in an area of his/her interest, and finally how they built a solid, sustainable and profitable business in the field. You come back enlightened and informed.

Which of the two approaches do you think makes a bigger impact on you? Obviously, it's the one where the acquaintance shared a powerful, relatable story of another person in the same situation. It helped you understand his/her point in a more compelling and effective comparison than with someone who offered plain facts, advice or suggestions. Stories play at an emotional and psychological level to move us. They are highly potent communication and conversation tools because they persuade people through examples. If I simply explain a concept to you, it may not have the same impact if I share an example related to the concept.

Stories increase your ability to connect with people. By nature, since evolutionary times, humans are wired to be more receptive to storytelling. The simplest way to pull someone's heartstrings is through storytelling.

However, through storytelling is a powerful technique of putting across your point more persuasively, not everyone is a wonderful storyteller. The good news is it isn't an inborn skill. Even if you think you are a 'low on confidence', ineffective and a rambling storyteller, there's plenty of scope for improvement through consistent efforts and practice. You may not be able to deliver the story with the intended impact or may take forever to get to the point. Whatever it is that you are struggling with – I've got your back here.

This book is designed to hold your hand and help you understand the finer nuances of being a master storyteller to increase your effectiveness as a communicator. It'll take your ability to connect with people in overdrive mode. With practical, actionable techniques mentioned in this book and its practice/implementation, you can be a boss storyteller. Everyone loves to hear stories, and acing this technique in communication can help you become an engaging conversationalist.

Let's nose-dive into the art of fine storytelling, and use it as a compelling conversation and communication element.

Chapter One:
Elements of a Compelling and Unforgettable Conversation

We agreed in the introduction how some of the most memorable and compelling conversations are the ones where the speaker strikes a chord with what he/she says. Some of the best conversationalists are those who can move people by sharing meaningful, relatable and identifiable accounts over plain facts and figures (which you can read about anyway).

What are these elements that make a conversation go from dull to dazzling? What are the elements that transform unexciting conversations into memorable interaction? What are the elements that make you go from socially awkward and ineffective to a persuasive and effective communicator? How can you distinguish between good/effective and bad/ineffective conversation?

Here are some of the most powerful elements of a good conversation.

1. Variety – This doesn't mean flipping from one topic to another frivolously without having deeper, more meaningful discussions about it. It simply means having an extensive topic bank to converse about. At a business networking event or social gathering, you are likely to come across people with varied backgrounds, interests, education, and competencies. You'll have to be able to hold forth on multiple topics if you want to wow them.

Keep abreast of the latest trends across several fields and topics. You will be able to travel effortlessly from one topic to another when people speak in a flow. If you are able to offer interesting insights and view on multiple topics, you are likely to leave a positive impact on the other person. Be an expert in your field of course but do not limit your interaction only to a certain arena, where you are an established expert. It'll make you come across as more one-dimensional with a limited worldview.

Smart, well-read people with a broader outlook and richer worldview are much sought after conservationists.

2. Timing – Timing is one of the most crucial elements when it comes to having a great conversation, especially for more impromptu talks.

You must be able to say the right thing during the right time or situation. You may want to strike a conversation with your new neighbor. However, if you see them walking towards their home soaked in the rain; you can't say "Hey, where have you moved from? What do you do?" and so on. The timing isn't right. During such times, it would suffice to say, "Hi there, how are you?" The timing is right for a quick ice-breaker and warming them up to you not having a long chat.

Similarly, if a person makes eye contact frequently, he/she may want to initiate a conversation with you. For instance, if you are in a bookstore and a person is constantly looking at the books in your hand or at you, he/she may want to chat up with you about your reading preferences or ask for recommendations /suggestions. Initiate a conversation such as, "This book looks fascinating. Do you enjoy reading autobiographies?"

Let's say you want to have a conversation with your boss or employer about a pay hike. Can you approach him/her at a time when they are preoccupied with work or exhausted after a particularly stressful day at work? Timing is critical when it comes to having memorable, meaningful conversations.

If a person talks about a death or personal tragedy in their family, you'll maintain a more somber mood. You won't take off about your promotion or celebrations. That'll be grossly insensitive and selfish, where you don't demonstrate concern for the other person's feelings and emotions.

Let's say you want to ask your best friend for a favor and know he/she isn't a morning person. You won't call them first thing in the morning and ask them for something. Instead, you'll wait until midday or early noon to put forth your request.

3. Compliments – Compliments are one of the surest and fastest icebreakers. They instantly help the person take a liking to you. People warm up and establish a connection. It'll also give you a base to build the conversation further. A majority of people react positively to sincere compliments. Try to stay specific, detailed and genuine while complimenting a person.

Our expressions and other non-verbal gestures are a dead giveaway when it comes to conveying our true feelings. If your compliments are insincere and vague, the other person will immediately know it.

Keep your compliments detailed, specific, well-thought and genuine to prevent them from coming across as plain flattery. Instead of saying something like, "that's a lovely outfit you are wearing" say, "I love how the cuts and color of your outfit flatter your body type and skin tone." Similarly, instead of saying, "You've done well with the latest project" say something like, "the latest project you submitted was very well-researched, especially the bit about the history of programming. I am impressed with your attention to details."

Often when we meet people for the first time and offer them compliments about their work (blog, thesis, papers, creative work and so on), we should be ready with specific compliments about some of the most striking elements of their work. For example, "I enjoyed your LinkedIn piece on how pessimism can help us become more productive and action-oriented. It was a unique and original way of looking at things, which helped me take back a few actionable points to boost my productivity." Contrast this with, "your LinkedIn articles are really good." The latter sounds like a more generic attempt at flattery, while the former sounds more well-thought and sincere! It demonstrates to the person that you read their articles and has your own take on it.

A genuine compliment also sets the tempo for further conversation. For instance, in the above example, you could build a conversation about the blog topic that you are referring to, and specify points that you could relate to and more.

If you want to make the conversation even more impactful and memorable, go a step further and ask the person for advice, suggestions, and recommendations. For example, "I follow your Tweets diligently and love your one-line reviews of new restaurants in town. Can you recommend a fuss-free café for an informal brunch with a friend?" or "I am thoroughly impressed by your presentation skills. The way you spoke about raising prices and global inflation, while addressing prospective clients is praiseworthy. Can you share some of your tips on putting together a powerful sales pitch?" See what we are doing here?

Offering the person a specific compliment and then asking them for advice, suggestions, and recommendations based on these compliments will completely floor the person. This will set a positive momentum for the conversation.

"I love your haircut. It is unique and flatters your face shape, do you have a preferred salon?" or "Your lunch looks creative, delicious and healthy. Did you make it? Would you mind sharing the recipe?" Ask relevant and interesting questions which build a conversation.

Find different ways to make an individual look good. Let the conversation be about the other person and not you. Make people feel wonderful about their selves if you want to create a memorable interaction. You'll come across as more likable and relatable if you make them feel great about themselves.

I happen to know a wonderful lady who is the founder of one of the largest Facebook groups in the world. She is popular and much sought after as a social media influencer. Brands clamor around her for promoting their products, and she has built a tribe of encouraging and supportive women. Part of the secret of her massive success is she never fails to compliment people, appreciate talent and praise people publicly. She has earned loyalty, respect and a huge following owing to her ability to make people feel wonderful about themselves.

4. Questions – Make your conversation a two-way process by allowing the other person and yourself equal time to talk and listen. If you go on speaking until eternity, the other person will get tired and most likely switch off. On the other hand, if you remain on the listening end, you'll not be able to share much about yourself and end up leaving a less than effective impression on the other person. Allow the conversation to flow naturally and effortlessly by transitioning from one topic to another smoothly or building on a single topic.

One of the best ways to accomplish this is by asking open-ended questions. If you stick to close-ended questions, the person may reply with a word or two and keep mum, thus leading to awkward silences. In place of, "It is nice and warm today, isn't it?" say something like, "How do you plan to make the most of this nice and warm day?" The idea is to prevent your conversation from reaching a dead-end. By asking open-ended questions you are allowing the person to offer a more detailed account, which can be built upon to create more engaging and enjoyable conversations.

Also, ask questions to demonstrate to the speaker that you've heard them out or clarify your understanding of what they've just spoken. This will make you come across as a more effective listener. For example, "I understand from what you've just told me that you are upset about not being given due credit for the project research." You'll come across as a more thoughtful and sensitive listener.

Ensure you ask intelligent, well-thought, relevant and meaningful questions over asking the obvious, which makes you come across as a dull and boring conversationalist. Being unique, original, well-informed and creative is the key. Use resourcefulness and presence of mind. Sometimes, you'll have to borrow clues from what the other person said (which means you have to listen keenly), and ask questions based on it. Other times, you'll have to pick cues from your immediate environment to pose a question to the other person. If you are tuned in to their actions, behavior, speech, thoughts, and ideas, you'll never run out of questions. Just keep in mind that it's a two-way conversation and not an interrogation. Allow the other person to ask you questions, and respond cleverly. The key is to enjoy an engaging and interesting two-way conversation.

I know people who love asking "if you could" questions to make the conversation more exciting and unique.

Questions offer insights and information, which you can use to take the conversation ahead. Ask purposeful and meaningful questions. Questions such as "What are career goals for the year?" Or, "What inspired you to quit your job and travel around the world?" Or, "What do you think about the latest (add trend within your industry)?"

Some people, especially those who are low on confidence or just acquiring social skills, might be more conscious when it comes to asking these rapport building questions early. Stick to simple, general and everyday questions related to the weather, hobbies, work and so on. Get to know the person better before posing more directed and deeper and purposeful questions. Reserve these questions for when you feel more confident about the other person's willingness to share more.

5. Common ground – You'll come across as more likable, identifiable and relatable if you are able to find a common link or ground for the conversation. This is especially true when you are meeting someone for the first time, and you want to leave behind a favorable first impression.

Try to identify common threads of conversation between you and another person. This may require practice and effort. You may have to work with different personalities and types of people. It may involve asking the other person plenty of questions to identify a common ground. However, it can be worth the trouble.

For example, you may be making an effort to establish a rapport with your new boss or potential client. You both may come from different backgrounds and have diverse interests. However, there can be that one small opening which you can identify and leap on during the course of your conversation. For instance, they may refer to a television show, a movie or a book they enjoyed reading. You may discover you have similar tastes when it comes to books, and get talking about books.

Some topics are always safe, and if nothing else you'll be able to relate to people based on them. For instance, everyone loves food. These are things that get a majority of people talking. Ask what their favorite food is or what they prefer eating for dinner to get the conversation rolling.

Observing people is integral to picking clues about finding a common ground. It can be a watch they are wearing, which gives you an opportunity to say something like, "That's a wonderful vintage watch you are wearing. Are you a fan of vintage watches as well? I have a sizeable collection of them." When they reply in the affirmative you can further ask them about their favorite piece and exchange conversation about vintage watches. Some of the best conversationalists are brilliant observers of people and human psychology. They are quickly able to spot unique and interesting things about people and identify common grounds to build a conversation.

"From the cut and fit of your suit, it looks like you prefer customized and tailored suits over ready to wear garments. I am a big fan of tailored suits too, where do you get your suits stitched from?" This is where your observation, compliment giving and questioning skills come into play.

You need to be able to look at the finer nuances of people's thoughts, ideas, appearance, clothes, personality and more, to come up with interesting and relevant conversation starters. Keen observation skills will also demonstrate to the other person that you are interested enough to listen to them or observe their actions, which is a huge plus when it comes to leaving a positive impression.

6. Call to action – One of the most common issues that people struggle with while making a conversation is how to end it with the right impact. My secret tip for ending a conversation on an impressive and memorable note is to include a call to action.

When I say a call to action, it may instantly up your sales antenna. "Hey, we aren't creating a sales pitch here", you may be mentally saying. However, ending with a call to action gives the person something to take back. It leaves the door open for future conversations and interactions. In essence, you are conveying to the person that the conversation is temporarily halted, and you'll get back to them for more.

At times, I've observed people end a dialogue or interaction on an awkward, unimpressive and stagnant note. They won't make the other person look forward to a conversation with them in the future or leave a flattering impression. Avoid leaving the conversation awkwardly, and make it more power-packed by offering the person a clear value or call to action. It should be specific and leave the person asking for more.

Say something like, "It was wonderful meeting you. I will keep interacting with you and would love to follow-up on the conversation we had today. Can you give me your business card?" Or, "It was lovely getting to know you, do check out the federation website I mentioned to contact influential people with your field." Give the person something valuable and useful to take back, which will make the interaction even more memorable for them.

7. Vivid descriptions – Vivid or detailed descriptions is what distinguishes average writers, writers, filmmakers, and other creative professionals from average to extraordinary. Doesn't someone who says "here's some liquid courage for you" come across as more interesting than someone who says, "Here's some beer for you".

Get more creative and detailed while naming or describing things. It is my single biggest secret to holding an exceptionally good conversation. Some of the most effective communicators use creative terms instead of the boring, usual descriptions. Replace the boring with more exciting, vivid and descriptive terms that paint a picture of what you are trying to communicate.

Advertisers and mass communicators understand the power of creating visual imagery through their words and phrases. It is the quickest way to play on a person's emotions. Listeners almost always take to visual imagery and emotion-laden words.

For example, instead of "it is so cold here" you can say something like, "My fingers are so frozen and numb, I can barely feel anything with them." In essence, you are conveying the same idea (it's very cold). However, the manner in which you are expressing it creates a difference in the impact.

Similarly, instead of saying "I burnt the pizza" you can say something more vivid, funny and interesting like, "I just burnt 700 calories in 10 minutes" or instead of saying "that's a massive pizza" you can say something like, "That's a heart attack lying on a dish" or "I am so stressed, I could do with a coffee", you can say, "I am dead tired, and need a chilled, decaf, whipped cream coffee." Do you get the drift?

It's expressing the usual ideas with a more unique and interesting touch using wordplay and creative expressions. Be more detailed and vivid while holding conversations. You'll come across as more expressive and persuasive.

Create comparisons and contrasts to make the conversation more exciting. For example, someone asks you, "How was your Paris trip?" You can reply with, "It was enjoyable" or you could say something like, "It was amazing because I didn't manage to trip and fall even once during my walks there, which in my own standards are rare and commendable."

The person will have no choice but to laugh. People enjoy listening to contrasts. It adds a twist to the conversation to make it more interesting. Mention an exception to create contrast, add clarity and include an unusual dimension to the interaction.

Notice how several television and radio personalities play with contrast to make their pitch even more interesting. They will seldom say anything like, "I think he's an exceptional dancer." Instead, they'll be likelier to say, "I think he's an amazing dancer. I am not saying he's Michael Jackson, but he has some really cool and classy moves. That's how they keep their listeners/viewers hooked and enthralled.

Similarly, a person may use comparisons to their advantage. "She's drop-dead gorgeous, probably the peak of gorgeousness, even more than the Kim Kardashian brand of gorgeousness." And we all know it doesn't get bigger than that, does it? You are taking your listener through a roller-coaster ride using comparisons and contrasts.

8. Nonverbal communication – Most communication experts agree that non-verbal communication is even more impactful and important when it comes to interacting with people than verbal communication. This is simply because it works at a deeper, subconscious level. Psychologists and master communicators have concluded that most people are drawn to folks who have energy and punch in their voice. Use your voice to your advantage for conveying the right ideas and expressions.

If you fill every word you utter with energy, everything sounds the same. The listener will not be able to differentiate between important and less than important points. Don't speak in a staccato-like monotone. Some things are as unappealing as a flat voice with zero expression or emotion.

Vary your tone to make it more impactful and energetic. Try to focus and emphasize crucial words. Use the power of silence to let the impact of what you said sink in. Give the other person time to process and comprehend the importance of what you just said. Vary your tone and volume to create a roller coaster effect with your voice, taking the listener through the highs and lows of the conversation. You aren't taking them on a boring ride. There are dips and highs coloring the conversation to make it more interesting.

Interesting conversationalists can vary their rate of speech to make the conversation more compelling and interesting. This works effectively because your speech and vocal patterns are often predictable. And we all know predictable equals boring and monotonous.

Divide your speech into chunks, and don't be afraid to pause for effect. If you want to communicate something important, try speaking in a slow and more paced out manner.

Learn to use inflection to pack more power into your message or lend it greater meaning. For example, ending your sentence on a high note may indicate a question, whereas finishing on a flat note may signal to make a statement or issuing a command. If you want to sound more confident or authoritative about something you've just said, end on a flat note or avoid speaking in a singsong manner. Keep your tone low-pitched and volume low to moderate to come across as effective communicators. People who speak in a loud and boisterous manner seldom get others to listen to them. Sure, you may grab attention, but it will be for all the wrong reasons. If you want to be heard and taken seriously, keep your volume low to medium, a steady/uniform rate of speech, a low pitched tone and clear inflection. The throw of your voice is crucial when it comes to conveying the right ideas.

9. Discussions instead of debates – I once met a highly argumentative person at the social gathering. He was arguing about everything under the sun and looked like he had a bone to pick with almost every person he interacted with. Needless to say, my brief interaction with him turned out to be nightmarish and left me drained.

Rather than engaging in a healthy discussion and dialogue, some people aspire to make every conversation a debate to massage their egos or enjoy a sort of one-upmanship over others. You will seldom win people or conversations by making people feel miserable about themselves. Avoid picking on people's comments and instead listen to them.

Admit you could be wrong to get them to drop their guard and become more receptive to your point of view. The conversation will become much easier and positive after this. No one wants to engage in a negative, draining and combative conversation.

Create a platform where both you and the other person feel comfortable about expressing opinions in a healthy, courteous and amicable manner. Arriving at a conclusion or mutual agreement on every matter isn't mandatory. If you can't arrive at a common agreement, disagree respectfully. Learn the knack of "agreeing to disagree" if you want to be a good conversationalist and communicator.

Chats, share opinions, discuss ideas, swap insight rather than viewing every networking event or social gathering as your battleground for pitting your stance against the other person's.

Avoid judging or criticizing people. Don't impose your views on others. Instead, stick to facts and figures to put across your point more scientifically. This will make you appear more objective and less biased. For example, let's say you are discussing vegetarianism with people. Instead of saying, "You non-vegetarians do not know the value of life. Imagine, killing a living being to satiate your taste buds. How insensitive is that!", say something like, "According to research, sticking to a vegetarian diet is healthier in the long run because you get more... and are less prone to... and animals aren't harmed in the process (this is just an example of putting across your argument)."

The other person will be more receptive to your ideas and views when you make your arguments more rational and scientific rather than emotional. You can start off by admitting up front that you could be wrong, and you'd like to examine the facts to correct your stance if it's incorrect. It will soften the other person's stance too, and they will also become more open to the idea of being proved wrong. Let things be open if a common consensus cannot be accomplished. Disagree in a polite, respectful and rational manner.

While a good conversation is about building on commonality, it is also about embracing differences. You will meet with diverse interests, backgrounds, political views, experience, religions, cultures, races, beliefs, ideas, and lifestyles. Look for a common ground, but also learn to celebrate and appreciate differences. Develop tolerance, respect, and appreciation for the other person's views or beliefs.

Concentrate on positive topics. It simply means instead of talking about past issues, regrets and controversial topics, stick to positive topics and future goals. Avoid talking about the coffee you spilled this morning, and instead talk about the inspiring book or movie you look forward to reading or watching post work. At times, it is alright to speak about negative issues. However, overall stick to positive topics. The negative topic discussion should have a clear objective. For example, you may want to bond with the other person by getting to know him or her more intimately, which may require a discussion of less than positive topics.

Always maintain a broader and forward-thinking mindset. It should be less cribbing and more solution oriented. No one enjoys being with people who complain all the time. It is draining. Focus on leaving behind an enjoyable, positive and inspiring impact on people. Stay less judgmental and biased, and more empathetic. Try to understand where people come from instead of harshly judging them according to your own beliefs, views, lifestyle, background and so on. It will help you become a better person to relate to.

Chapter Two:
Use the Power of Storytelling to Connect with People

"After nourishment, shelter, and companionship, stories are the thing we need most in the world." - Philip Pullman

Stories are a wonderful medium for expressing not just your views, but also complex ideas, values, experiences, and thoughts. They impress people and establish a human connection. While facts, figures, and statistics adopt a more scientific and rational approach, stories tug at people's heartstrings! Facts are a more clinical and mechanical way of conveying ideas, while stories are more relatable. The listener or audience can relate to people and experiences in the stories, and hence understand what the speaker is trying to communicate even more effectively.

As human and highly social creatures, we respond positively to stories. Everyone loves to hear an engaging and powerfully narrated story.

Why is storytelling an important medium of communication?

All of a sudden, stories have made their way into the world of marketing, business, and promotions. This is partly owing to the explosion of social media, where brands focus on creating engagement through connections. Stories have, since time immemorial, been a part of our society and cultural ethos. Even as children, if our parents or guardians wanted to persuade us into doing something, the stories were their best weapons.

Stories are omnipresent – they are all around the place, from books to movies to news channels to history. As a communication tool, stories are probably as old as humanity itself.

Did you know that 90 percent of buying decisions are emotionally influenced? This means engaging prospective customers or clients by establishing a human or emotional connect is integral to the process of persuading them to buy. This is exactly why you'll find plenty of commercials and sales pitch with compelling visuals, fascinating products descriptions, photos, and often a relatable story thrown in for good measure.

Notice how the pitch of almost every internet marketer who claims to have mastered a system or promises to make people 'millionaires' has pictures of shiny, luxury cars or private jets, a big house, beach vacation pictures (where they are sipping on an exotic drink) and more. The pitch begins with how they started with nothing and didn't even have enough money to buy food for the family when they lost their job. Then goes on about how they discovered or invented a system that completely transformed their life. Why do you think they share all this? It's to make their pitch more emotion-laden, identifiable and connection-worthy. While reading it, you may say, "Hey that's me. I can also be a millionaire like Joe or Jill. If he/she can do it, so can I." Then you go about signing up for their program because you want a life like theirs.

The internet is filled with stories of internet marketers and bloggers. What makes case studies so effective from the business point of view? It is nothing but a company's story, which tells you how they tackled a particular challenge or what they did differently or how they used something to their advantage or the strategies they used to grow their profits. It helps other businesses and budding entrepreneurs sit up and take note, "Hey, we are sailing in the same boat, we can use these principles to grow our business too." Get the idea?

If you want to be an effective communicator, you should be able to weave storytelling into your conversation or speech to establish a connection with your listener or audience. As a salesperson, you should be able to use the power of storytelling to impress your prospects. You can attract people like magnets once you master the art of narrating compelling stories.

Ask yourself this question. You are impressed by facts, but do you connect with them on an emotional level? Chances are if you start by reading an article containing facts and figures, you won't even recall most of it by the time you finish reading it. Do we remember numbers and facts on our fingertips? Rarely! Now contrast this with a powerful story you read at the beginning of an article. Will you remember it by the time you finish reading it? Most likely yes! Humans remember stories more effectively than facts.

According to research, stories trigger positive emotions are more extensively shared than those stimulating negative emotions and feelings. Notice how content that generates higher emotional arousal almost always goes viral or is extensively shared. This simply means that stories that help people experience a positive feeling or emotion, such as wonder and happiness are more likely to do well than stories that make people feel angry or depressed.

Like it or not, stories are most often more powerful than anything you can say. It can make or break the point you are trying to communicate. This is because stories evoke feelings. We all know the potency of feelings and emotions in the process of communication. If I ask you to go back and think about teachers, educators, mentors, and professors who left the most positive impact on your academic and personal development, you will most likely name people who narrated a lot of stories. This is because you remember the lessons they imparted through stories more effectively than someone who stuck to plain facts and figures without reaching out for your emotional chords.

Stories add more punch to your message. For example, let us say you are talking about the power of good customer service. Instead of simply saying how important good customer service is in today's age of social media and the internet (which everyone knows fairly well), if you narrate a story about how a family's vacation was ruined when they were thrown out of the flight an airline because they wouldn't give up seats they duly paid for, and how they took on the airline on social media to create negative publicity about the airline, resulting in tremendous support for the family and loss of business for the airline, you will put across your point more compellingly. Examples and stories move people.

There is a difference between telling people that some airlines will go out of the way to serve their passengers and narrating a story about how an airline turned around the aircraft to ensure a passenger slipping into coma gets quick medical attention. Doesn't the latter convey the same message more effectively? It moves you or evokes certain feelings about great customer service. Feelings are very powerful when it comes to communicating your point or persuading people.

According to research conducted by Jerome Bruner, we are 22 times more likely to remember a piece of information/fact, if it is presented in the form of a story. That makes stories pretty powerful tools if you want people to retain information. You probably remember only those lessons from the school where the teacher weaved a powerful story around a concept, incident or idea he/she intended to teach. It's like packing a lot of information into little packages with fancy wrappers –all condensed and easy to consume.

Think of your favorite television series and movies. What is it that you love most about them? Most likely their stories! The stories are designed to help you enjoy or relate to the characters and/or situations. You probably identify with the characters or relate to them at some level. We are aware that these characters are fake or it's a fictional account, yet we cannot help but identify with them owing to the emotional resonance.

Have you seen the Airbnb ads as of late? The company doesn't tell stories of its customers. They let their customers themselves share accounts of how they experienced a destination like a local rather than a visitor. This enhances the brand experience of a place like a local feel, to make Airbnb come across as a brand with a genuine human touch. This is the power of stories.

Facts may help you tell, but stories manage to sell. By acing the art and craft of storytelling, you spark people's interest in a way of thinking or brand. This happens through connection and engagement. Draw people compellingly into the narrative with your slick storytelling skills. Have a clear purpose for narrating any story.

Which of these do you think will have a greater impact on say a person suffering from a terminal ailment? Statistics about how many people suffer from the same ailment survive or a story about someone who suffered from the same ailment and how they overcame it? You know the answer!

Whether it's a fictional novel, movie or a friend narrating his/her experience, everyone is captivated by a good story. Have you ever wondered though about why we feel engaged and persuaded by a powerful narrative?

It isn't tough to understand. Let's say you are listening to a PowerPoint presentation being delivered by your project leader or manager. There are lots of bullet points throughout the presentation. This stimulates specific regions in your brain referred to as the Broca's and Wernicke's area. On the whole, it works on our language comprehension brain regions, where we are able to give meanings to words. That's about it.

However, if your manager narrates stories throughout the presentation, things change drastically. It not only stimulates your language processing parts, but also other brain regions that we utilize when we are actually undergoing an experience similar to the one being narrated. So your brain processes the story as if you are actually going through it.

For example, if the person is talking about how beautiful or exotic vacation destination is, our sensory cortex gets activated, and we are able to 'experience' the place in our mind as if we are actually experiencing it in real. Similarly, if the person speaks about speed or motion, our motor cortex gets activated.

Why do think metaphors win conversations? Apart from the speaker's creativity, it allows the listeners to live things through sensory experiences. If you talk about an opera singer who has "a satin voice", you are triggering your audience's sensory cortex. Why do you think writer's use sentences such as "She gasped for breath", or "His cheeks became hot and flaming red with rage." It triggers the reader's sensory cortex.

One of my friends began her career as a teacher at an elementary school. She spoke about how things belonging to grade 2 students went constantly missing from class. It happened on several occasions, and she realized that a student from the class was stealing other children's things. She addressed the class on more than one occasion urging whoever was doing it to return things belonging to others as it was wrong to take what belonged to other people.

When this didn't work, her mentor suggested that she use the power of storytelling in helping the child mend his/her ways. My friend then went on to narrate a powerful story about how stealing was morally wrong, and how it impacts the person who steals and the person whose things get stolen. The next she found all the stolen belongings kept on her table before the class began, and the errant child even confessed and apologized to her saying they would never touch things belonging to other people ever. The child grew up to be someone the teacher is very proud of today. Imagine the impact of a single story on the child's character and persona.

What Are the Basic Elements of a Good Story?

We'll take an in-depth look at the elements of a good story in the next few chapters, however, let's shed some light on the fundamentals for starters. Now just because I say storytelling is a powerful form of communication doesn't mean any story will work. There are bad and ineffective stories too that do not add any value to the message you are trying to convey. Create engaging, appealing and powerful stories is also an art and requires practice and consistent efforts. However, like most things, it isn't impossible. Here are some basic elements of a good story that can inspire your listeners or audience.

Character – The most important element around which

any story revolves is the character or characters. There are powerful and compelling characters in any good story or at least they become powerful in the end. This character helps establish a connection between you and the listener. Picking characters that resonate with your audience is the key to getting this element right. Choose a character or characters your audience or listeners can identify with or relate to on a personal level.

Remember the internet marketer's example I shared previously in the chapter. The reason they are killing with their products and services is that people can instantly relate to their stories (whether these stories are true or false can be debated, but the idea is people buy their stories before buying their products or services). Someone who has lost their job or is struggling to make ends meet or feed their family identifies with the marketer's struggle. They may see themselves as ambitious, driven, and harboring aspirations of a desirable lifestyle just like the internet marketer. Hence, they may relate to these marketers at a personal level through the latter's stories.

For creating/narrating about a character your audience can easily identify with, you need to know your target audience thoroughly. You need to know their problems, desires, demographics, aspirations and more. For example, an internet marketer may realize that his/her target audience mostly comprises people who aren't too happy with their jobs and are looking to make a full-time passive income from the internet for greater financial freedom.

They may then share stories about how unhappy they were working for someone else's dreams and empire rather than building their own. How they got fed up, and quit their jobs and how it's the best decision they've ever taken in their life. They'll go on about the financial freedom they currently enjoy, where they have plenty of money and the time to enjoy that money. When you know more about the listener or your audience, it is easy to weave stories around characters and situations they can relate to.

Drama – A good story almost always has an element of drama. It can be a conflicting situation or a dilemma that matches your listener's situation or dilemma. It can be an event or experience they went through.

You can weave an element of drama in your stories by identifying your audience's or listener's needs, journey, experiences, and problems. They will find it tough to connect with the story if the drama doesn't fit their needs, desires, conflicts, and experiences. Listen and tune in to their desires and problems of your target audience or listeners. An element of drama or conflict helps create a powerful emotional connection with people.

In the above example, people identify with a situation where a person has lost his/her job and is unable to care for their family at an emotional level. They will think about their own family, and their desire to give their family a better life. This helps them establish an emotional connection with the narrator. Ensure your story has drama, but it should also be realistic and genuine. Notice how salespeople or marketers make preposterous claims in their sales pitch stories come across as fake, and have you running for cover. Drama should be genuine, and not overdone. Keep it natural, realistic and relatable.

Resolution – Where there is drama, conflict or a challenging situation, there has to be a resolution. It's the way a story flows organically. Powerful stories are meant to surprise us even if they do not always end on a happy note. The resolution should provide a logical conclusion to the story, and ideally should move people into action. A good resolution is the one that gets them thinking. It makes them feel about something and inspires them to take action in the same direction.

Going with the same example, as a person who has just lost their job, after reading about how an unemployed person went from being penniless to a multi-millionaire, I may feel hopeful and inspired about accomplishing the same. It may get me thinking about how "I can make big money too." This may get you to act on starting your own business.

Before you narrate or create a story, model your character on your target audience, build a powerful emotional appeal, be genuine while creating a conflict situation and finally tie it all together with an authentic resolution. A clear, easily understandable and concise story almost always wins the day.

> *"Your purpose is to make your audience see what you saw, hear what you heard, feel what you felt. Relevant detail, couched in concrete, colorful language, is the best way to recreate the incident as it happened and to picture it for the audience." – Dale Carnegie*

Chapter Three: Weave Stories Effectively in Conversations

"The universe is made of stories, not of atoms." – Muriel Rukeyser

In the mid-18th century, British politician John Montagu, the 4th Earl of Sandwich enjoyed playing cards in his free time. He also relished snacks, keeping a hand free for holding the stack of cards. Eventually, Montagu hit upon the idea of eating his slice of beef by putting it between two toast slices so he could keep a hand free for his cards. This meant he could comfortably enjoy his snack and play cards together.

Eating his newly created "sandwich", the name given to two bread slices with vegetables and meat placed between them became one of the world's most sought-after inventions. Now, it's very likely that you will never forget this story about the invention of the sandwich. Imagine having a conversation about a person at a party about sandwiches, and slipping this story in between. Doesn't it make you come across as an interesting and compelling communicator? Now, contrast this with simply stating facts about sandwiches. Is the person likely to remember it? Slim chance.

I always recommend having a nice bank of these trivia stories ready as party conversation starters or a way to impress people with your knowledge. It can be a lifesaver when you have nothing else to speak. Some topics are safer than others. For instance, good food! Everyone loves good food, and when you don't know much about a person's preference or their personality, these stories make you come across as an interesting and engaging conversationalist.

Who remembers bullet points and information-based content in conversations? Striking a rapport with the other person becomes easy and effortless with stories and anecdotes.

The left brain communication style, which appeals to people's sense of logic doesn't work very effectively in today's world. If you wish to communicate your point in a compelling, persuasive and powerful manner, you more or less have to employ the right-brain communication approach. People today communicate through the medium of stories, which is easier when it comes to conveying ideas, feelings, and emotions. Stories lend more authenticity to your message. Authenticity, genuineness and a human connection are what most people and brands are looking to establish in a world marked by frenzied competition.

More than 27,000 years ago, since cave paintings first came into being, narrating stories have been an integral part of our communication process. It is a science and art. It remains one of the most effective ways to start, build and end a conversation until date. Here are some tips to use the power of storytelling to make your conversations more effective and impactful.

1. Tell stories with a clear a takeaway – The listener should be able to take back something valuable from the interaction. This will only come once you know what is relevant and crucial for the listener. For example, someone talks to you about a fear of switching careers, you narrate a story about someone you knew switched careers successfully and are today glad about their decision. The story ends on a happy note with the protagonist being happier and more successful after switching careers. It gives your listener a clear takeaway – this may be a risk worth taking or people have done it successfully before me. Take time to think of, or create stories that will have the intended impact on the listener. The emotion or feeling should stay behind with the listener long after the story has ended. Have a clear purpose of narrating the story and give your listener something valuable and interesting to take back.

2. Great stories are about challenges or struggles – Let's go with the above example where you are talking to a person about switching careers. If you simply list the pros and cons of switching careers, he/she won't be likely to listen to you or may not recall the conversation. Chances are he/she has been offered several opinions and views. However, when you tell a powerful story about how someone transformed their life by overcoming a challenging situation or conflict by swapping careers, he/she will relate to the conflict as if it is their own, which will make the conversation even more impactful and memorable. There has to be an element of conflict that the listener will identify with to offer him/her hope that he/she can tackle the challenges in his/her life as well. People identify easily with how other people reacted to the conflict or challenging situation they currently find themselves in.

3. Keep 'em short – This is especially true if you are conversing with a person for the first time. When you don't know much about a person, do not bore them with long-winded and wordy accounts. Grab their attention and spark their curiosity with short, concise and powerful stories. They shouldn't be longer than four to five minutes.

At times, in a bid to not give up conversing with the other person you tend to go on and on with the story. You make it much longer than they need to be in your zest to be in-depth. A compellingly summarized 500-word account can be more impactful than a superlatively written 3,000-word essay.

Don't use stories to fill tip or make up for awkward gaps. Use them to drive home the intended point. The objective should be to entertain, entice and captivate your audience. I am not asking you to omit crucial points from the narrative, but don't spend an hour needlessly establishing the background. No one has the time to listen to long-winded stories, especially in one to one or group conversations.

4. Always imagine your story to be a motion picture – You are the screenwriter of the movie with the intention of conveying your message powerfully to the audience or listener. Much like movie stories, your story should have a clear beginning, middle, and an end. It will most likely begin with the protagonist and his/her challenges. This will be followed by intensifying the reader's interest and curiosity by including vivid descriptions about people, places, characters, and human emotions.

5. Get creative – No one likes to listen to stories which have been narrated a million times. Your stories have to be unique, interesting and creative. I know a person (a fun and engaging conversationalist) who creates storyboards for every occasion, so he has a story to narrate for almost every situation or emotion. In his free time, he'll draw characters based on something he observed or read. He'll then create highs and lows around the character, basically, the full-fledged emotional arc that is integral to the art of storytelling. He knows exactly when to pull his listeners into the story, introduce elements of tension and conflict (much like those fairy tales with monsters and princesses/damsels in distress). Needless to say, he is the center of attention at most parties and social gatherings. If you are creating your own stories to suit specific situations, ensure they sound realistic and authentic. Build your stories a manner where they are able to convey the intended meaning.

6. Deliver the story powerfully – The best stories will fall apart if they are delivered in a weak and monotonous manner. Include variation in your voice. Use intonation, pitch, and volume to your advantage. This is where your narration skills will come into the picture. How you deliver or present a story is as important as the story itself. If you have to touch the other person's raw emotions, you've got to use your verbal and non-verbal communication skills effectively.

For example, when you want to make an important point about how something won the day for the protagonist or how he/she overcame a particular challenge, you may want to say it and then pause. Pausing allows the other person to process and ponder over the impact of a powerful message you just conveyed. Contrast this with following up quickly by saying something else instead of pausing. You haven't allowed the magnitude or intensity of what you said just to sink in. Allow the other person the time to feel the intended feelings and emotions if you want the story to have the desired emotional impact.

Pepper your stories with metaphors and idioms to make your language even more vivid and sensory. Allow people to visualize and experience your stories at a sensory level. Metaphors, similes and other figures of speech convey an idea more vividly because they activate a person's imagination which is integral to the process of listening to a story.

Include richer imagery, more detailed descriptions. A "short, stocky and chubby woman with gray hair, wearing red stilettos was walking towards me" creates a more detailed visual imagery than a "fat, old woman wearing heels was walking towards me." Create a detailed and more descriptive imagery to keep your listener hooked. They'll most likely hang on to every word you say and seldom leave the conversation until you've wrapped up the story.

As far as possible, use direct speech while narrating the story. Avoid reported speech. She screamed, "What are you doing here?" sounds much more impactful than, "She asked me what I was doing there."

7. **Be a reader and observer** – It isn't a secret that you need to be a highly resourceful, creative and imaginative person to be a master storyteller. You need to have a rich and colorful vocabulary of words. In addition to this, you must be able to know how to use phrases, expressions, idioms and other language elements to your advantage while narrating stories. This comes with reading books and observing people/other speakers while they are speaking. Observing people also helps you sketch characters in your mind in a more detailed manner

– with their typical mannerisms and quirks.

For example, if you observe how musicians, rock stars or live performers typically behave when they are meeting or greeting their fans, you'll be able to create a more vivid and detailed account of their character while narrating stories about rock stars or live performers and their interaction with fans. Being a good observer and reader is integral to being a master storyteller. Start observing things, people, places, and situations around you if you want to develop your storytelling skills.

Reading helps you develop your language, narration and imagination skills. When you read stories, you learn not just new and clever ways to convey everyday ideas, but also different narrative styles and ways to trigger the listener's imagination. An author who is articulate and has a brilliant sense of expression inspires you to create your own vivid imagery while narrating stories.

Details are important in a story. However, as a narrator, you'll have a take a call about how long or short you want the story to be. If you are conversing with a person you've just been introduced to, you may not want to bore them to death with lengthy accounts. However, if you are addressing a group of mentees and trying to teach them a powerful business lesson, you may use long and detailed stories. In personal one to one conversations, keep your stories brief and impactful, unless the listener is demonstrating a keen interest in listening to detailed accounts. You'll know through their verbal and non-verbal expressions whether they want you to go on or stop. Use these clues to cut short your stories or make them more detailed.

8. Practice storytelling sessions and conversations with a familiar person – One of my favorite tips for being a master conversationalist and story-teller is narrating a story before a mirror. It allows me to focus on the delivery or story narration. For example, how I sound while saying certain words, the voice and intonation, my body language, expressions, pronunciations and articulations, and much more.

You can also practice narrating these stories to a friend and a trusted person before using them in social scenarios. Test it with a friend or family member to gauge their reaction. If they are blown away by your narrative, it'll most likely impress others too. Urge your friends and family to be honest and genuine in their feedback. If a story doesn't move them or have the desired impact over them, drop it.

Get feedback about your narration pace, while making a note of the story's length, language and narration style. Do not be discouraged if your storytelling is a bit raw and rusty initially. It comes with practice because below the surface, humans are born storytellers. It's the way we are wired. Once you get into the groove of things with practice and effort, storytelling will become second skin – smooth and effortless.

9. Begin with a hook – Understand that storytelling in conversations in different than sharing stories as part of a public speech or official presentation. It's more informal and laid back in a conversation.

Begin by hooking your listeners with the main point. The beginning and end should include the main idea. Get people engaged with your basic point, before they feel compelled to hear the rest of your tale. In technical terms, it is referred to as a hook. It helps the listeners or audience determine if it is worth investing time and effort listening to the story.

For example, "My boyfriend went to the car wash day before yesterday. He normally does the car cleaning chores himself, but this time he wanted a more professional job done and was also running short of time."

What is the problem with this hook? It doesn't manage to captivate the listener's interest. As a listener, you wouldn't want to listen further. What's so extraordinary about a guy who normally washes his own car getting it professionally washed for a change because he running short on time? There's no hook and no one's listening. Tough luck!

Now, look at this opening.

"You should have seen my partner's car interiors after it came back from the car wash day before yesterday. He usually cleans it himself, but that particular day he decided to…"

You are more or less saying the same thing, but the second introduction is more hook-worthy. It entices the listener and makes them want to listen further. The beginning also conveys the essence of the fundamental point of your story. Without a powerful hook, you fail to grab your listener's attention. They'll quickly move on to talk to someone else.

Quick, fast-paced sentences are effective story openers. Think something dramatic and swift such as, "I almost died after that car rammed into me", or "I saw something really peculiar last night." It's like a signpost that'll convey to your listener that you may have a story to tell or something interesting to share. At times, people may not show a keen interest in hearing your further, nor may verbally/non-verbally offer clues revealing their unwillingness to listen to you. Don't stress about it too much, and stop. It may not necessarily mean you are an ineffective narrator. The listener is probably tired or is uncomfortable discussing a particular topic. This may not be the best time to share your story or anecdote. Leave it for a more appropriate time or switch to another topic.

Also, learn the art of responding to people's anecdotes if you want them to respond favorably to yours. When a person shares a story or anecdote, acknowledge it by injecting more feelings into your reaction such as, "Oh dear, I can't believe you were abducted by a gang a few days ago. It must have been terrible." Or, "Wow, the way you saved the day for your boss and organization is commendable."

Offer verbal acknowledgment in the form of appreciation, shock, amazement, surprise and so on by using appropriate language expressions. Complement this with the right gestures, facial expressions, tone, and body language. It is important for the speaker to know that he/she has created the intended/desired impact over you through the story or anecdote. I also like asking people questions related to the story or anecdote they've just shared to reinforce my interest and understanding. It tells the speaker that you've been listening to them in a focused and interested manner, which instantly makes them take to you.

Effective listening is a huge component of being a competent communicator. Social skills and communication aren't simply about talking nineteen to a dozen for impressing people. It is always about lending a patient, empathetic and keen ear to others. When you make interactions more about other people and less about yourself, you win.

10. Does it have an entertainment value? – Keep your story or anecdote in social conversations extra short if it doesn't offer much entertainment value. I know plenty of people who exaggerate, especially while narrating personal anecdotes. However, avoid lying and misleading people. Exaggeration for the purpose of increasing a story's entertainment value is fine as long as it doesn't mislead, misinform, harm or hurt people. The intentions behind exaggerating the story are what matters. Imagine how ridiculous you will sound if you narrate a story about being abducted by extraterrestrials when you clearly weren't. As much as possible, keep your accounts genuine and authentic, especially in informal social conversations.

Typically, you should also be able to signal to your listener or listeners that the story or anecdote is completed. This can be done by saying, "that's it", or "that's all that happened", or "and that's my alien encounter story." Like you offer a signpost before beginning a story, offer a signpost after concluding the story. At times, the listener may think you have something to add to the story or may not realize that it has wrapped up. This is when a clear "story has ended" verbal signpost gives them the idea that you've finished narrating.

Chapter Four:
Elements of a Powerful Story

We briefly discussed the elements of a good story in an earlier chapter. However, here we take a detailed look at what a distinguished story bore people to death from stories that make them sit up and notice. If you use these elements in your storytelling, you most likely have listeners hanging on to every word you speak and go back with the intended objective or impact.

Here are the elements of a powerful story.

1. The dramatic aspect of your story should be strong – You can't weave a story centered around on the idea that "a person eats eggs and ham for breakfast." Will it grab people's attention? No! Why? Because it doesn't say anything extraordinary. Millions of people around the world have eggs and ham for breakfast.

Now contrast this with, "a person has eggs and ham for breakfast, but no one knows the ham is made of human flesh." Eek! Now, this is story-worthy. It instantly sparks your attention and probably very strong emotions. You are repulsed by the idea. It's dramatic and sensational. A story should have an element of drama to grab people's attention and intrigue them. They should want to know more about it. If you talk to me about a person eating human flesh for breakfast, I'd obviously want to know more about it. Drama packs the required punch in your tale.

We've all heard how a dog biting a man isn't newsworthy. However, a man biting a dog becomes breaking news. You have to create drama by weaning in the unexpected if you want people to be hooked. There has to be an element of shock, surprise, novelty or sensationalism to grab the listener's attention. A story or anecdote will seldom be interesting for the listener in the absence of drama.

What are some elements that can be used to create drama?
- Surprise, shock or sensationalism
- Suspense
- Tension
- Challenges
- Out of character human behavior
- Unusual occurrences or events that do not usually occur
- Controversy
- Mystery
- Conflict

The example we mentioned about human flesh comprises a majority of these elements. A majority of people find cannibalism repulsive. It is out of the ordinary behavior for a person to consume human flesh. It is a highly sensational and controversial matter. There are tension and suspense (someone has been killed obviously). You want to know about this mysterious person who is consuming human flesh.

I am not implying that drama always equals disturbing, shocking, sensational and controversial content. It can also be a small detail such as whether an employee who pretended to be loyal yet went on a stealing rampage throughout the office was finally caught. Do you get the idea? Build drama around your stories to make them more interesting.

There has to be some sort of turmoil, struggle or challenge that leads to a more positive and hopeful resolution in the end. Drama makes the other person want to listen to you further. "I met a terrible accident a few years ago, and was unable to walk." Now the listener is captivated because he/she wants to know how you overcame the situation. Conflict takes your story ahead. Compare these two narratives.

"I completed my graduation with top honors and took up a well-paying job in the banking sector. Owing to my diligence and hard work, I was quickly promoted to the position of an assistant manager. Then, I became a manager owing to my leadership, people development and mentoring skills. Later, I was promoted to the position of a senior manager. Today, due to my people skills, hard work and sincerity, I am General Manager of business banking."

"I completed my graduation with top honors and was employed by a top banking for a much-coveted position. Soon, owing to my hard-work and diligence, I was promoted to the post of an assistant manager. This was followed by two quick promotions to the level of manager and senior manager. I was slated to be at the top of my career when I lost my limbs in a freak accident. I was unable to walk for more than a couple of years. Life came to a standstill. But not the one to give up, I picked up the pieces of my life once again. With the help of artificial limbs, I began walking and going to work again. It was tough in the beginning. Sitting for long was a challenge. I began to feel depressed and irritable. However, my co-workers were a huge support. They supported, encouraged and inspired me to do my best. Here I am today, General Manager, business banking."

Which of the two stories has a greater impact or is more moving? Obviously the second one! The story has a clear arc. There are highs and lows in the narrative. It starts on a positive note, followed by a tragedy or personal conflict, finally ending with a resolution. It takes the story ahead or gives it the so-called a 'twist in the tale.' The former doesn't have a narrative arc. It is flat, an all-positive story that is devoid of challenges or conflicts. The end doesn't resonate very well with the viewers because it's flat-out boring. Nobody gets into trouble or faces a challenging situation. There is neither an internal or external conflict. Everything hunky dory doesn't make for a good story.

2. Create memorable, identifiable and realistic/believable characters – This is huge. It can make or break your story, and/or its intended impact. Why do we remember some characters over others? Simply because they have a unique persona intriguing/perplexing motives, unusual flaws and/or strengths or they have a very distinct appearance (notice how while talking about a person, we may not remember their name but we can describe them vividly to help the other person understand whom we are referring to).

Would you remember the characters in your story if you stood in a queue after them for 10-15 minutes? What makes the people in your story so special? While using characters in your personal conversations, seminars, business presentations, and other situations ensure you keep them relatable and identifiable. Yes, there has to be an element of uniqueness and novelty, but people should be able to relate with a "youngster just out of university at the crossroads of life, not knowing what career to pursue." There should be something about the character that resonates with people at a primal, emotional level.

If you want your listener or audience to relate to the

character on a personal level, never forget to share their origins. "So I came across this young boy who attended one of my seminars. He came from a small English village and was eager to live the American dream. His parents were farmers and couldn't give him the best life. However, he managed to get scholarships and earned his degree through sheer determination and hard work."

You are creating an inspiring character by referencing his background, which lends greater context to the story. An audience comprising people who have small-town origins and plan to get a degree may identify with the youth mentioned in your story. Establish the character's motives, goals, objectives, and purpose throughout the story. It'll make these characters come across as more connect-worthy and relatable. When people connect with your characters on an emotional level, you've won the audience.

Pay attention to details about the character if you want to make them more memorable. For instance, "The lad came up to me and said I want to make it big in life" doesn't have as much impact as, "The tall, lanky lad walked up to me and almost yelled in his typical regional Yorkshire accent that he wanted to make it really big." Focus on the character's expressions, quirky traits, slang and much more to make your description more interesting and identifiable. When it comes to stories, the good is truly in the details.

How does the person look? What was he/she wearing? What was the color of their eyes – all this can add more interesting dimensions to the story. Of course, it will eventually depend on the type of audience you are addressing, the purpose of storytelling, the available time and more. However, detailed stories make a more memorable impact (since they create more vivid sensory experiences and are retained in the mind) than stories that simply skim through the surface to convey general ideas, thoughts, and emotions.

Relatability is a huge factor when it comes to moving or persuading people with stories. Avoid using far-fetched and out of the world characters that the listener or audience struggles to relate to. There should be a common connect, something they identify with at a deeper level. The listener should be able to identify with the character or feel that this is them or something they are going through in their life. It increases the impact of your narrative. Create situations that your listener can effortlessly relate to.

3. The opening should be attention-grabbing and dazzle worthy – A powerful story instantly captivates your attention and makes you want to hear more. A good opening should be like a teaser. It should tantalize listeners with partial information. You whet their appetite and leave them hungry. Make them wait eagerly for the tale to unfold. Leave them gasping for more.

Take this opening, for example, "I walked into a room full of people who couldn't stop laughing at me." Now obviously as a listener or an audience member, you want to know why people were laughing at the narrator. He/she has grabbed your attention with a teaser opening. You want to know how the narrator found himself/herself in the middle of a potentially awkward situation, and the events that followed.

Avoid opening your stories by stating the obvious or ordinary if you want to pull your audience or listener into the narrative. Consider the impact of an opening like, "I am a university professor, and begin my lectures at 8 am each morning" What is so striking or intriguing about a university professor beginning his/her lectures at 8 am each morning? As an audience, you'll be like, "come on now, please get to the point quickly." It makes you bored and impatient. There's nothing arresting or unusual there. In fact, it is downright dull.

Use an opening that sets the right tone, momentum, and rhythm for the story. You won't obviously reveal everything there is to the story in the opening, but you'll set the theme so the listener more or less knows what to expect.

There isn't a thumb rule for powerful openings though in general, they should be slightly extraordinary, surprising or shocking. At times, depending on the situation and people, you may have to play down some elements. Use your people reading and intuitive skills to know how to open a story for making the desired impact. Different people respond differently to different scenarios. Use icebreakers with your listeners or audience to get a feel of their likes and dislikes. You don't want to offend or annoy them with your opening. Similarly, you don't want the opening to be weak and ineffective either.

Instead of making abstract points that few people are able to comprehend at the beginning (you'll leave the majority feeling that the story is not for them, and they'll quickly switch off); the opening should be clear, intriguing and brief. Don't lay down all your cards at the beginning of your story. Give people a reason to sit back, and listen. Also, there's no rule that stories should always begin from the beginning if you know what I mean.

You can cut forward to a recent incident and then go back to later events. This makes your narrative faster paced and interesting. Remember, your opening sets the tone for the rest of the story. Make it compelling and attention-grabbing.

Another thing is that most communicators fail to grasp is to have a unique voice while opening and narrating stories. You should have your own distinct narration style that is different others, and your opening should sufficiently convey this.

For example, wry humor may be one narrator's style, while the other may use sarcasm. Another story-teller may be downright hilarious and vivid in their descriptions. Some storytellers thrive on descriptions and detailed observations, while others love to pepper their stories with smart one-liners. Identify your style based on your objectives and personality, and keep it more or less consistent throughout the story. Develop a clear narrative to distinguish yourself from other storytellers and conversationalists.

If you use too many different styles throughout the story or open using one style, and quickly to switch to another, your listeners may feel exhausted and annoyed trying to keep up with multiple styles. Ensure your opening line or lines establish the narration style you plan to use throughout the story.

4. It has a valuable takeaway – Good stories always help the audience leave with a valuable take away. To convey the truth or facts you can use charts, statistics, graphs and bullet points. This will establish the truth scientifically, but may not move your audience or listener into taking action or give them something valuable to ponder about. Stories, on the other hand, can work on raw emotions. For example, let us say you are talking to an audience, person or group of people about greater customer service. You are trying to awaken them to the importance of exceptional customer service in today's competitive business world. Let them go back with an actionable, clear and practical solution with a story.

Now you have two options. Either list all characteristics of a competent customer service professional (you should be this and that, etc. to be a great customer service professional) or narrate a powerful personal anecdote mentioning how you went out of the way to serve a customer in need.

You are leaving your audience with a powerful takeaway, about what good customer is. They understand and implement your suggestions even more effectively. You have not just told them what to do, but also presented an example of how it is to be done, and given them clear pointers to take home. It inspires them to offer good customer service, and create a positive overall experience for buyers. A personal anecdote clarifies exactly what you are trying to convey.

Chapter Five:
Pointers for Narrating Powerful Anecdotes

We all agree by now that stories and anecdotes are the lifeblood of our social interactions. They not just enliven any conversation, but are also responsible for our collective community values and ethos. We connect at a deeper level with other people through the power of stories. An anecdote is a short, simple story that we tell people on an everyday basis while chatting with them. It can be an incident that occurred to us or something that happened to a person we know or a childhood memory. At times you tell someone how something that happened to you taught you an important lesson.

Since anecdotes by their nature are not as structured as regular stories and are more ubiquitous, the narrator doesn't put in a lot of effort in mastering the storytelling art and craft. You won't practice narrating an anecdote. You may just come across a situation at a party and narrate an anecdote related to it. It's more spontaneous and spur of the moment than practiced and rehearsed.

What makes anecdotes so appealing? When you are attempting to establish a relationship with people, it is important to keep them engaged, entertained and informed. Anecdotes do all this and more.

Fundamentally, anecdotes are brief accounts or narratives of true stories involving us or other people. Narrators are generally the protagonists in their anecdotes, and they are used more in casual, social situations, though there is nothing that stops people from using it to make official speeches or presentations more entertaining.

Notice how you'll be talking to a person you've met at a party, and they'll start telling you about an incident involving traffic cops that happened on their way to the party. The purpose is to inform, amuse, entertain or make you aware of something. Anecdotes add more a more interesting dimension to your social interactions. These are stories you share to reveal your personal side in social situations. People get to know more about you in an entertaining manner.

Think of the difference between telling a person you enjoy playing golf and narrating an account where you developed an interest for golf and how you recently won a local golf championship tournament. The latter will be more evocative and interesting in communicating your passion for golf.

Entertaining people make them develop positive feelings

towards you. When you make others in a conversation feel good, they are more inclined to trust you. Don't you relate better to people who share fun and interesting personal information about themselves? Also, anecdotes are a wonderful way to get people to share a bit about themselves too. When you share personal information or accounts about yourself, you are opening the door to let the other person share interesting personal information with you, thus paving the way for a meaningful and memorable interaction.

The popularity of anecdotes is at an all-time high owing to social media. It's an age of short, pitchy narrations that grab people's attention while establishing a connection with them. We have in effect become quick-cut dialogue makers. Say something quick and effective, and move on! Each time Facebook asks you, "What's on your mind?", aren't you tempted to share something that happened on your way to the gym or while driving to work?

A major difference between anecdotes and stories is that anecdotes relate to facts – "We dropped little Joshua to preschool this morning and it was raining heavily. We were already running, the car broke down on the way, we got completely drenched and fell sick." It is a narration of facts as they happened. Some people love to add drama by exaggerating it (when it becomes more of a structured story). But by and large, anecdotes are about facts.

On the other hand, a story generally has a more structured beginning, middle and conclusion. While an anecdote entices, a story offers enticement and insight. It gives you something to reflect upon in the end.

To create an effective dinner party or social gathering story or anecdote, think about an incident which you have an overpowering urge to describe to other people. I don't know if it has ever happened to you, but a lot of times when something interesting happens with me, I feel compelled to describe it to others. Think of such instances. There may be incidents that friends ask you to share several times. Give it more thought. Flesh it out into an arresting anecdote with more value and meaning.

However, there are powerful tips to perfect the art of narrating anecdotes. There can never be definitive techniques for something as personal and varied as storytelling. However, there are lots of proven methods that can help you become a better conversationalist by peppering your interactions with interesting and engaging anecdotes.

Here are some of the elements of impactful anecdotal stories.

1. Link them to a value after defining the stakes – In any gripping anecdote, the subjects either gain or lose. The anecdote falls flat on its face without this element. You'll come across as dull and boring if there's nothing at stake for the involved parties. Now, this shouldn't lead you to stretch facts or resort to lies. Simply understand the objective of narrating the anecdote. Why are you narrating this specific anecdote in the context of your conversation, training or speech? What do you hope to gain from it? What will your listener/listeners take back from it? Once you decipher all this it is easier to organize your thoughts.

Are you trying to communicate a value? Are you trying to acquaint the listener/listeners with values such as loyalty, punctuality, friendship, honesty? Link the value or the lack of this value to the stakes within your anecdote. For example, how a person lost something because of dishonesty (lack of value) or how an employee gain something because of his/her loyalty (presence of the value). Connect the winning and losing closely with the values (or lack of them) that you intended to communicate. By linking the stakes to clear values, the canvas of your anecdote will slowly begin to emerge.

For instance, let us say you are having a conversation with some people at a social gathering about parking authorities, and someone comments about how unfair and 'on the prowl' local parking authorities are. You wholeheartedly agree and think of sharing an anecdote about a recent incident that reinforces this view, and how you responded to it to escape their malpractices. Now, you have a rough framework of the story.

The initial view is the local parking authorities are unfair.

The value response is you must be on guard and alert all the time, including watching out for the meter time, status tags, your civic right and more.

The reinforcing scenario is something that proves the original view that the city's parking authorities are unfair, where you had to suffer or bear the consequences of not being aware and alert. Here, the stakes are the consequences you had to undergo. It could be having your car forfeited for a day or pay a hefty fine.

The value assertion is another situation, which also reinforces the original view. However, this time your actions can be slightly different. This time you are aware of the authority's malpractices and create a plan to foil it. Their regular traps fall flat. As a result, you save yourself from the negative consequences that you'd have to otherwise suffer.

To convey your point even more effectively and make things more gripping, you can increase the stakes within the second scenario by not only talking about the fines and impounding act but also running late for a crucial job interview. You added another stake to make the anecdote even more compelling. So the stakes aren't just limited to the authority's unfair practices, but also another negative consequence you had to endure as a result of it or managed to escape owing to your presence of mind.

Finally, the payoff is the lesson, value or moral of the story. In the above example, it is about the importance of being more alert and aware of the malpractices of local parking authorities. You can end with something memorable and feel-good, such I managed to make it in time for my date, and I am now married to him/her.

You've now built the framework, an original view, engaging stakes, and appropriate values that characterize great anecdotal pieces.

2. Begin the action – At the beginning of an anecdote, we are only too tempted to invest more time offering unnecessary introductory information. This makes the anecdote lose its power. In the absence of action, it'll most likely fade into oblivion. Let us compare two openings here.

"I am a public relations professional. I frequently have to wait until my clients come to me with assignments. During one such waiting period, I was chatting with a close friend who is also my legal consultant. We were having coffee at a local café when I received information on an assignment to cover a brand in Los Angeles. My friend thought the entire thing didn't sound too genuine and asked if he could accompany me. We rented a convertible, packed in a lot of hard liquor, and took off for the job."

I bet you won't be able to go beyond the first few lines. It is downright dull and unimaginative. There is no action. The only thing remotely arresting here seems to be packing of hard liquor while setting out for a job. Why not begin with the interesting part then grab the listener's attention? If you insert it in the end, the listener may switch off before you reach the end.

Now compare this with the following paragraph.

"I don't know where we were, but somewhere in no man's land en route to Los Angeles. The liquor had begun to take its toll. My friend started saying, "I feel giddy. Maybe, it isn't a good idea for me to drive." This was followed by an ear-shattering sound around us, a terrifying roar!"

Begin with action so you have the listener's attention and then go about weaving in other details instead of making it a boring account filled with unnecessary and unimportant details. As a listener, you'll be bored to death if you have gone over a detailed account with no action in sight. You'll be waiting for something to happen, but the story doesn't move ahead with the appropriate action.

Avoid being hung up on unnecessary details. Look at the lines below. "It was an early Tuesday morning when we came across a strange smell emitting from the door to the other side of the hall. Hold on, it's a Wednesday. It was early Wednesday morning. No, that doesn't feel right either. Was it actually a

Tuesday, Wednesday, or Thursday morning?" As a listener you want to scream, "How does it matter? Go on and tell me what that strange smell was!" Unless you are writing a novel, it doesn't really matter!

I mean these details would be vital to the story if you're crafting a murder mystery or establishing an alibi timeline, etc. This isn't about the murder investigation, timelines, and alibis. Don't fret about details when it comes to anecdotes unless they are integral to the story. If you can't recollect anything, leave it. If you can, mention it. Anecdotes are seldom about these details.

Take for instance you are sharing a childhood experience or incident. Will the listener care if you get the day or month right?

3. Avoid getting verbose or diatribe – There are some instances where it's fine to rant. Think political speeches, election campaigns, lecture hall, television debates and so on. However, they are meant for a clear purpose. However, social or dinner table conversations over drinks don't necessarily have to polarize people, bore them to death or embarrass them. Try not to divert yourself from a great story by ranting or making it a verbose account.

You can duck plenty of uncomfortable situations by avoiding controversial rants. Try avoiding them, and listeners will more often than not ask you for more insightful, engaging and interesting experiences. There's something about sharing anecdotes that help people go back with a powerful takeaway. It makes you a far more engaging conversationalist than sermonizing or stating facts. Focus more on the impact than details. What emotions are you trying to awaken in people? What is the feeling you are attempting to communicate? Are you getting them to feel fear, happiness, frustration, helplessness, danger and so on? Focus on putting across the right feeling rather than being stuck with details.

Some of the best anecdotes are those that allow the listeners to experience the exact same feelings you went through when the incident/anecdote you are narrating occurred. Describe the events and experiences that made you feel the emotions you want to activate in your listeners. Keep it short, impactful and simple. Each time I find myself in a situation where I am stuck with details while narrating an anecdote; I simply say "anyway" and move on to focus on the emotional impact or main matter.

Your objective should be to get everyone together not polarize or break people apart through the anecdotes.

Also, avoid showing off. No one enjoys being around social peacocks who don't connect at the human level. People may listen to you to get you off their back quickly, but they'll seldom connect with you at a deeper level if you come across as a conceited person or show off. Even when the stakes are pretty high, do not be afraid to reveal your vulnerability. People who make their selves look slightly silly, almost always win it over those who fake perfection. You may not have the most serious conversations with people by revealing your silly or more vulnerable side, but you'll manage to break the ice, and that's huge! Conversation starters are critical, and some crack-in can help you.

4. Have a precise and clear ending – Your anecdotal story should offer a closure to the listener. It's not a murder mystery series where you leave with a cliffhanger. Wrap all the loose ends logically in the end so it all adds up and there's closure.

Don't allow your ending to meander all over the place or allow it to halt in the middle of nowhere. You'll most likely leave your audience feeling cheated for giving you time and attention. Even if you don't have the answers, try ending with details you know for sure. Throw in a provocative question for good measure. Leave behind a solid impact even if can't answer all questions. At times, creating an alternate ending or hypothetical closure also works in the absence of all available answers. You can then logically transition into another topic.

5. Write it – Some people find sharing an anecdote easier if it's written. This is especially true for people who are not very confident or awkward when it comes to striking a conversation or approaching strangers. They'll often think they are not good storytellers, wonder what their audiences will think or whether their stories will have the desired impact. Think about the objective of the anecdote, and start writing in a journal.

List some of your favorite anecdotes, and make an effort to use them throughout your conversations and interactions. Edit wherever required according to the tips mentioned in the post. Your anecdotes will develop a greater level of clarity, fun and engagement value.

You can use these anecdotes everywhere from job interviews (yes they are sure to win any interviewer who has to sit through a hundred drab interviews throughout the day) to wedding toast, cocktail parties, or business networking events. This fleshed out a variant that you have just written will come to you easily and more confidently because you've already written it once. Your story will leave people dazzled, and create the intended impact. Winning and re-telling anecdotes will become easier when you write them in a more structured manner. You'll develop better storytelling skills in the long run.

6. Find the perfect moment – Anecdotes are generally narrated during more informal, social sharing sessions. Don't push your anecdote into the conversation simply because I've told you it makes you come across as an interesting conversationalist. It should add value to the overall conversation and sharing. The subject of your anecdote should be relevant to the general feel and the topic of your conversation. If the topic revolves around inflation, and you narrate an anecdote that highlights your luxury travel experiences around the world or the problems in today's education system, it just doesn't make sense. You'll only come across as insensitive to the topic of discussion or plain irrelevant. Don't use anecdotes to hijack or force a conversation. There are appropriate moments and topics to share in your anecdote. Your anecdote should add value to the conversation.

For example, let's say someone is talking about the challenges of finding a suitable rental accommodation in the city. This is when you can share an anecdote about painful experiences with your landlord. Similarly, when someone speaks about impolite and inconsiderate customer service by the airline staff while traveling, you can share your experiences with rude airline personnel.

At times, socially awkward people are not very comfortable opening the topic for discussion, yet they are eager to come across as engaging and entertaining conversationalists. In such a scenario, initially let other people take the lead when it comes to picking a topic for discussion. Follow this up with your own anecdotes when they finish speaking about a topic. This way, you won't feel pressurized to initiate a topic, but will still add to the conversation in an engaging and meaningful manner. Find an opportune moment to jump in, and make the most of it.

7. Use the appropriate narrative tenses – A majority of times, we narrate stories and anecdotes in the past tense, like something that occurred in the past. You can use simple past, past perfect or past continuous tenses for your narration. Here's how you can best use these tenses. Past simple can be employed to explain primary actions in the fundamental part of the story.

For instance, "I saw a huge spaceship descending to the ground, and halted my car. The objects around me started floating automatically. I witnessed a dazzling light flash, and before I knew it awoke in a forest with excruciating body pain." Past simple tense is generally used when you have to convey shorter and more impactful or shocking scenarios. These are fast-paced and more unexpected actions that happen in quick succession.

Now if it's a more elaborate moment to moment action, you may have to adopt past continuous as your narration tense. It is also used to elaborate on the situation when the primary events occurred. Past continuous lends context or sets the scene for the anecdote. For instance, "I was driving late in the night through the countryside when I spotted something rather unusual." You are creating a setting and context for the events to unfold.

When two events occur at the same time, past continuous tense is used for the longer event or action. The longer action begins, followed by an interruption by the briefer past simple event, and finally, the longer continues if required. For example, "I was attempting to recall where I was when suddenly these people in gray suits showed out of nowhere and began asking me personal questions."

Past perfect is generally used for giving a backstory or background to the main anecdote. Employ past perfect tense when you want to refer to events that happened before the main action or event in your anecdote. For example, "I narrated about how I had been camping in a tent bang in the middle of a forest and that I'd awakened to visit the toilet, and couldn't locate my tent. That is why I was sleeping under the tree. I told people how I hadn't spotted any aliens or anything similar." Past perfect isn't easily noticeable by the listener. The "had" is slightly contracted and can be easy to miss.

While past simple is the most common tense form used for narrating stories and anecdotes, past continuous and past perfect lend it greater depth, layers, and range. Practice using a combination of these three tenses in varying degrees to improve the impact of your narration. Think carefully about how they can be employed to describe various events in the story or anecdote.

Chapter Six:
Using Storytelling for Sales, Business and Professional Networking

A story can literally sell for you. Yes, this isn't an overstatement or exaggeration. You can carry an entire sale based on a single, powerfully narrated story. You don't believe me? Have you seen the 80s blockbuster Top Gun? It is about two dashing and dapper naval pilots who are offered the opportunity with the best pilots on earth at the much sought after "Top Gun" pilot school. It was the ultimate sales letter anyone could ever write

Why do you ask?

Ray-Ban Aviators sold like crazy, witnessing a whopping 40 percent increase in their sales figures. Air Force and Navy recruitment soared. It sold the idea that it's cool to be a fighter pilot, so much so that recruitment booth had to be set up in theaters screening the movie. This is the power of a well-told story in selling.

Did anyone in the movie urge the audience to buy the

sunglasses or join the Air Force/Navy? Both these products/ideas were more than successfully sold to plenty of people. How can this be applied to your promotional and marketing efforts?

Ask any successful salesperson the secret of their success and they are most likely to reply with the fact that they don't sell but establish a rapport with their prospective buyers. Instead of simply selling, they help their customers buy. Storytelling contributes majorly to the rapport building process. It makes the salesperson come across less of a machine parroting the features and benefits of his/her product and more human, likable and relatable. Why do you see a sudden surge of advertisements and promotions where people are offering a first-person account of their experience with the product? Think Dove and other brands.

While rookie salespersons will focus on the product features, benefits and functionality, veterans will concentrate more on building a relationship through personal stories and anecdotes with their potential clients. You don't drive sales by talking non-stop about the product. Sales are driven by more emotional, impulsive decisions, which are a direct result of tugging at people's emotions.

For instance, if you narrate a story to a mother how a product related to children benefitted another child; she will be driven to make the purchase decision for her child at an emotional level. People care less about the products and more about people. If they can establish a human connection with you, they're sold.

The best salespeople are ingenious storytellers. They know how to weave artistic tales around the big picture or their customer's biggest problems, fears or aspirations. These people know how to gradually but surely draw them into a narrative about a sophisticated solution for their problem. Some of these people will not even speak about the products or services until several meetings. They will offer details only when they are certain the client is hooked and refusing is not an option.

Let's look at an example. Say you are a salesperson selling a bulk emailing software. It's a fully loaded, complete bells and whistles product that is ideal for your email marketing campaigns. You approach new and established companies with your world-class application.

The wrong pitch would definitely be how wonderful the product is, its inbuilt features and so on. Honestly, there are a thousand similar products and the client cares a lark about your bells and whistles. You are doing nothing but adding to their confusion of whom to purchase from. Thus, to prevent themselves from making a bad decision, they will most likely not purchase from anyone and wait for the noise to settle. Bad for you!

Contrast these accounts how your last five customers clocked a 10x return on their product investment because they were able to target several email users ethically. When you offer case studies or examples how someone in the same industry achieved a result the prospective client is struggling to accomplish in specific terms, you've slain it. Think about this, an employee will want to buy the application to appear smart and solve his/her organization's problems.

Have you spotted the difference? In the earlier example, it was all about your products and services – its features, benefits, uses, etc. In the second, it is about your customer or telling them stories about how other clients solved similar problems using your products and services. You will almost always win people when you make things about them and not about yourself.

In the latter example, you grab their attention by clarifying metrics about their enterprise to help prospective clients paint a more vivid picture of what they can expect after using your products or services. In comparison with merely telling them what they can accomplish, you are demonstrating what they accomplish through examples. It is also more attention-grabbing when you tell them how it is going to be a huge financial victory for them in the long run. Minimize their risk of appearing foolish by buying your product, and instead narrate a story or example to show them how it's one of the wisest decisions they can ever make. Do your homework before approaching clients. Figure out what exactly the client wants before you approach them. What are the main pain points? What are they seeking a solution for? How are you going to tackle their main pain points? How are you going to appear smarter by offering your prospective customers an elegant solution to their problems?

Think of yourself not as a salesperson, but as a competent creator such as William Shakespeare weaving a tale or Da Vinci create artistic brush strokes. In essence, people don't like to be sold to. They want people to find solutions for their problems. Stories and examples make them feel like they are accomplishing a personal win, wielding a clever decision or solving a clear problem. The more effectively you weave a story with the given pain points and needs, the higher are your chances of getting the customer to take action in your favor.

Personal stories and testimonials have a lot of power when it comes to selling. It is of little wonder that you have brands clamoring to you for sharing your experiences with their products and services. It is fairly easy to strike a chord with prospective customers using personal stories.

The method is simple. Take the people step by step through a challenge that you encountered, and how you managed to accomplish desired results that the prospective customer is looking for. Share a personal story to establish a connection with people to essentially tell them that you were sailing in the same boat as them, and managed to find a solution to their problem. Instead of telling them how they can accomplish the desired result, tell them how you did it.

Let us say you are selling an acne reduction cream, you can talk about your own painful experience with acne. What it was like to live with a sensitive skin or acne breakouts? You'll probably talk about the pain, hurt, rejection and humiliation you went it. The personal account will have the emotional, physical and psychological ramifications of acne. How you tried different methods but nothing gave you relief. Talking about the horrors of living with acne will help prospective customers (people suffering from acne) identify with your pain. Then, finally, you'll talk about how the product you are selling (acne cream) brought you the desired result.

See what we did there? We wove a story around your personal experience rather than simply listing the features and benefits of the product. You shared your own story that will resonate with people suffering from acne. It makes you more identifiable and relatable as a salesperson. You aren't just selling a cream, but selling hope in the form of a product by narrating a personal story.

Like I mentioned earlier, purchase decisions are almost always driven by emotional impulses. The prospective customer is sold if you are able to tap into their inherent emotions through the power of stories. You take prospective customers through the highs and lows of your experience with acne to finally end on a positive note, which makes them feel that there's finally a remedy for their acne problem. Take them through the worst of the problem, while finally leading them to how the issue was resolved. You are likely to close your sale in no time.

Another trick is to use stories that make other people feel good or special. Some of the world's best business, sales, and political leaders realize the importance of telling stories that make other people feel good about themselves to sell products and services. These stories may have an aspiration value attached to it.

How do you think travel and lifestyle brands manage to clock heavy duty sales even during a recession? They tell stories about people fulfilling their dreams, accomplishing a better work-life balance, achieving their financial goals and in general living a fuller life. Give people hope and aspirations through stories. Make them feel good about themselves.

Sales and marketing people who show a keen interest in people's lives, their success and overall well-being almost always manage to close the sale. Discover the prospect's interests, passions, preferences, background, views, fears, and aspirations to weave a story around it. It becomes easier to connect with them when you have more information about their "hot buttons" or what drives them. Once you have this valuable information, it will be easier to weave stories around their "emotional drivers."

One of the best sales tips I've picked up is to remember details about your previous interaction with a customer, something most salespeople usually don't. The prospective customer will not expect you to remember tiny details of your previous interaction.

Sweep them off their feet by recalling something they said earlier or letting them know their preference for so and so. They'll almost always buy from you. By remembering minute details of your previous interactions, you are making the other person feel valued and special. On a psychological level, this instills feelings of likeability towards you. Once you become likeable and relatable, they're likely to take action.

In sales, stories act as a social proof. Humans are social creatures. When they realize someone like them is doing something to eliminate or reduce challenges they themselves are facing, they are likely to take action in the desired direction. It's a bandwagon effect.

Let us say for instance you are trying to sell an expensive set of encyclopedias to parents. Now, if you simply tell them that the books are invaluable sources of knowledge for their children, the printing and pages are high quality etc., they won't be as impressed. However, try rattling off the names of people in the neighborhood who've purchased them and how their children have benefitted from it (shared in the form of feedback) and they'll be likelier to think "Oh! I don't want my child to be left out."

The herd mentality rarely fails when it comes to getting people to do what you want. Use the power of stories to make people aware of how others are benefitting from something, and if they don't want to be left behind, they take quick action as well. There is a deep, subconscious need to be like everyone else, which makes us want to fit in. Use stories that tell prospective customers how they'll fit in perfectly with your products or services.

I once had a salesperson approach me for selling customized children's storybooks. I'd never even heard of them until then or knew they existed. The storybooks have your child's name as the central character, which is guaranteed to make reading more enjoyable. Your child obviously feels special. Since I wasn't familiar with these books, I hesitated in making a decision. The salesperson then launched into a narrative about how other co-workers and neighbors have ordered these books as exclusive and unique Christmas presents for the children. He even went on about how parents who were initially hesitant were delighted with their children's response and reading habits and went on to order even more of these books.

Now, that really got me thinking. I began by thinking it was nothing much than the usual commercial, Christmas time hypes. I am certainly not paying that much for my child to read a story that's been read a million times just to see her name in print. However, hearing detailed stories about Mr. And Mrs. XYZ purchasing these exclusive presents for the children made me feel why shouldn't I gift my child something special, unique and exclusive? Why should I deprive my little one of this wonderful experience when all other children will enjoy it? I know examples and stories are a clever sales manipulation technique, but I couldn't help it and be still sold. I didn't want my child to be left out.

Let's say you want to dine at a fancy restaurant on a first date with a person you've been crushing on for long. There are two amazing fine-dine restaurants you've zeroed down on but can't seem to make up your mind over which one to pick. You browse through Yelp and realize that while has bagged several positive reviews for the food and service, the other has more than a few accounts of how the restaurant ruined a perfect date or anniversary celebration due to bad service. You'll obviously stay miles away from the second restaurant. Why do you think reviews are so effective when it comes to making purchase-related decisions? Reviews are nothing but personal feedback and stories about people's experiences or stories about the product or service, which help you decide whether it is suitable for you. Stories are a form of validation that other people have used or are using something successfully.

Using Anecdotes in Speeches and Presentations

Move over ultra-futuristic animated, presentations packed with data, and welcome powerful, simple, clear and effective anecdotes to articulate your point. You really don't have to be a Silicon Valley head honcho to deliver a powerful speech or presentation. All you need is a clear, appropriate message, and a few amazing stories or anecdotes to illustrate it. Focus on a single theme to make the delivery more impactful.

Instead of reading facts and figures, where the human connection is lost, identify a key message and weave some effective anecdotes around it. This is the shortest and best way to make any speech or presentation go from boring to dazzling. If you have actually experienced something, you will be able to convey it with authentic feelings and emotions. You'll be able to narrate your experiences as if you are living those feelings and emotions, which come across as pretty powerful to the audience.

Stories are sticky content. People will almost always remember a well-told story because at a certain level, it arouses strong feelings, and leads to the release of dopamine in the brain. This is precisely why stories stick in our memory far longer than facts or figures. In short, making people feel something is one of the best ways to make them remember the point you are trying to convey.

Think of your stories and anecdotes as comprising three acts. The initial act is where you propose or present an idea, setting or situation that is created to engage the audience. Use something that has happened in the past which is of greater interest to your audience. The ideal, it should be related to a problem or challenging situation they are currently facing. Use the information that they aren't aware of.

For example, "Our buyer numbers have been plunging since the last 15 quarters, and today I learned that it's officially down for the 16th quarter. We just cannot function like this anymore. There, now this is a problem they are facing, coupled with attention-grabbing information."

In the second act of the story, you simply lift the stakes of the initial idea you intend to communicate. It should be something that can't be undone. "We are going to have to shut the manufacturing units in Sacramento and Boston."

Notice how you are separating your story into distinct parts to create the desired impact. This is the basic structure of a good story or narration.

The third act of the story proposes a resolution. It is generally favorable. To turn this grim situation on its head, I am introducing a promising new line of products that will be a hit among our customers. It will get them crowding back into all our stores. You don't announce that you are resolving the situation or offering a solution for the audience's troubles. You convey that through your story or anecdote.

The most effective resolution is when you can get the audience to take action by pulling them into the momentum of a highly persuasive moment. "I have placed a product from our new line under each of your chairs. Please feel free to try them."

This is pretty much the basic structure of a good story. You begin with a challenging issue or an unknown piece of information to grab the audience's attention. This is followed by magnifying the problem even higher to create a compelling story arc in a speech or even conversation. Finally, you come up with a resolution or get the audience to take action in a positive direction.

Now there are certain categories of stories in western society that can be effectively used to drive people into taking the intended/desired action. For instance, let us say as a business owner, project leader or manager you have to urge your team to embark on a challenging task of creating a new product. How responsive to do think they will be? It's a long, tiresome and arduous journey. They'll most likely crib about the long hours, low pay, higher stress, and other challenges along the way.

However, if you narrate a quest or mission story the Wizard of Oz or Holy Grail, you'll most likely tap into their subconscious mind to see themselves as heroes on a mission, where they emerge triumphant despite obstacles. They think of themselves as central characters in the story of their life, and how they win against all odds to accomplish their goals. This is how stories can be used to work on the audience's subconscious and unconscious feelings and emotions. You are invoking thematic concepts and ideas through the speech to impress people and get them to do what you want. Never make the mistake of presenting yourself as the sole hero of the story. Always involve your audience. They should be able to view themselves as extraordinary too, if they have to take action in the desired direction.

There are typical story categories that powerful orators use. Think rags to riches story.

Using Story Telling in Training

Let's say you are training a group of innovative and strategic customer service solutions. You talk to them about different ways through which you can deliver a world-class customer service experience. However, the group will most likely forget a majority of customer service ideas and solutions you discussed during the training.

Contrast this with a story. Each time my friend Jill faced an issue with her hosting service, she would contact the customer support team of the host company via live chat. Each tweeted about one such communication with the support team (nothing extraordinary a lot of people tweet these interactions if they happy or angry at the end of it). What did the web hosting company do next? They sent Jill the very same neckpiece she had pinned on her Pinterest board since long. Needless to say, the hosting company won a customer forever. Jill wasn't just happy about their resolution, but also surprised at the touching gesture. She completely forgot about the initial technical issues she faced with the company.

Do you think the group will forget this story? You've got them thinking about turning around a potentially negative customer experience as an opportunity to leave them floored. This is more powerful than any discussion about the elements of good customer service.

Think about how effective stories can be on soft skill development and other training. Want to talk about faulty time management? Cinderella to the rescue!

At times, stories help make the abstract more concrete. Resistance to change often comes from being unsure of how to proceed. For example, let's say a person is aware he/she should eat healthy food or exercise. However, it is an abstract piece of information. How can it be converted into something more practical and actionable? A story about how a person's healthy eating and exercising schedule can show them exactly how to do it, thus clarifying an abstract and vague piece of advice. It puts into perspective or context, how the advice or information can be practically used which bring down inaction barriers.

Conclusion

Thank you for reading or listening to this book.

I genuinely hope it has offered you plenty of practical and actionable pointers to increase your confidence, and elevate your social conversations to the next level through the art of storytelling.

The objective of the book is to help you get rid of your inhibitions and to take on the social world by conversing in a more confident and effective manner by mastering storytelling.

The next step is to start using the strategies mentioned in the book right away to be a powerful communicator, storyteller, and people magnet.

Finally, if you enjoyed reading the book, please take the time to share your views by posting a review on Amazon. It'd be greatly appreciated!

Printed in Great Britain
by Amazon